COACHING AND MENTORING

KEEPING IT SIMPLE

JODIE DAVEY

Published by Write Angles Press in 2025

Jodie Davey ©2025

A catalogue record for this book is available from the National Library of Australia

A CIP catalogue record for this book is available from the National Library of Australia

ISBN: (print) 978-0-6459237-9-7

(ebook) 978-1-7642378-0-2

Cover and inside pages design by Claire McGregor (https://clairemcgregor.com.au)

Editing by Kellie Nissen (https://justrightwords.com.au)

Disclaimer

ACKNOWLEDGEMENTS

*Once again, I wish to acknowledge my husband Steve –
for your continued support in all I do, your patience when I
am struggling and the pride you show when I achieve.
Over twenty years of marriage, you are my rock and my
best friend. Thank you*

*To the incredible people I have met and worked with for the
past eight years with Powerful Partnerships. My journey as
a coach and mentor continues to develop as I learn from
each of you. Maggie Lloyd, Susan McRedmond, Dr Shyam
Barr, Kellie Nissen, Dannielle Charge – just to name a few.*

*To my beautiful sisters, Angela and Karryn. We continue
to feel joy in each others' successes, and I'm truly blessed
to have you in my life. Keep being you and leaving your
mark on the lives of others.*

WHAT PEOPLE SAY ABOUT JODIE

From whole school professional learning, team and executive level coaching, Jodie's expertise has been a game-changer. Staff have grown in confidence as collaborators amongst parents, students and each other. They have developed strategic thinking and through Jodie's work, positively impacted school culture and wellbeing as a team!

Allison Edmonds – Principal, Turner School, ACT

I was fortunate enough to work with Jodie after a particularly difficult phase of my teaching career. I had immigrated to Australia from South Africa and found the challenge of assimilating to a different system in a different country particularly tough. After a year of struggling, I was left deflated, with little to no confidence and seriously questioning whether or not teaching was for me. Fortunately, Jodie came along and was employed as my School's Head of Teacher Performance and Development. This was absolutely life changing for me. Jodie took me under her wing, she listened to me, comforted me when I cried or when I felt anxious and slowly but surely helped me to find my love of teaching again. Most of all, Jodie, with her calmness and kindness, helped me to find my strengths and recognise that I was capable, competent and qualified. She gave me back my confidence. Working with Jodie gave me reassurance and helped me to build on the skills I already had in order to become a better teacher. Her approachable manner and nonjudgemental approach meant I never felt afraid to ask for help or admit when I was struggling – a difficult thing to do in the high-pressure environment of a private school. Jodie was able to foster an environment of acceptance and support which allowed me the space to make mistakes and then learn from them – steps we all know are vital to success in the classroom. I will forever be grateful for Jodie and her mentorship. I would not be the teacher I am today had it not been for her kindness and compassion and her guidance and leadership. I am not sure I would even be in the classroom at all had it not been for Jodie's mentorship.

Kelly McBean – Head of House, Senior English Teacher

Jodie Davey has played a significant role in my professional growth for over a decade. Our journey began when I was a classroom teacher, and she coached me with kindness, humour, and unwavering professionalism. Jodie has an exceptional ability to ask the right questions at just the right moment – prompting deep reflection and ultimately helping me improve my practice. As I transitioned into leadership, her coaching and mentoring and leadership workshops equipped me with the skills and confidence to support the growth of others. Now, as a principal, I continue to benefit from Jodie's guidance – not only personally, but also through the support she provides to our entire staff during her regular visits. Her wealth of knowledge, experience, and storytelling continues to inspire and uplift our team. Simply put, Jodie's Powerful Partnerships approach has been instrumental in my development and that of our staff, and I am deeply grateful for the ongoing support she so generously offers.

Megan Worthington – Principal, Redeemer Lutheran College, QLD

Having a mentor like Jodie in the early stages of my teaching career was essential to both my success and my wellbeing. For young teachers, it's crucial to have the freedom to grow and make mistakes. They need a space where they can have open conversations about pedagogy, behaviour management, parent relationships, and organisational strategies, without the fear of judgement.

Jodie created that safe space for me and my fellow new teachers. Her professional expertise, organisational skills, and genuine passion for teaching made all the difference. I am incredibly grateful for her support, knowledge, and the kindness she consistently shared. To this day, I continue to learn from her example and feel inspired by the generosity and wisdom she brings to everything she does.

Nikki Dunn – Senior Teacher, Assistant Head of House

ABOUT THE AUTHOR

I began my teaching career in 1992 as an enthusiastic 20-year-old, fresh out of university and full of energy. My first posting was in a small country town in South Australia, where I spent four wonderful years teaching in primary schools. Though teaching wasn't something I had seriously considered during high school, I quickly discovered a deep passion for the profession. I was excited and fulfilled, and I genuinely believed I was making a difference in the lives of my students. The classroom felt like home.

In my fifth year of teaching, I was posted to a city school where I took on the role of Curriculum Leader – my first experience in leadership. Just six months later, I was invited to step in as Acting Deputy Principal for the remainder of the year.

Over the years, I continued classroom teaching across a diverse range of settings – international schools, Catholic schools, state schools and independent schools – in both primary and secondary environments. Each experience enriched my practice and deepened my understanding of teaching and learning. Although I held several leadership positions during this time, my heart remained in the classroom. I took immense pride in the impact I was making on the thirty students in front of me every day.

Then one day, everything shifted.

I began to see leadership through a new lens. No longer was it about stepping away from the classroom I loved – it became an opportunity to extend my impact. I realised that by leading and supporting other educators, I could indirectly influence the learning and lives of many more students. This was my light-bulb moment. I knew I was ready to become the kind of leader I would want to follow.

Over the next twelve years, I embraced a variety of leadership roles: Assistant Principal, Curriculum Adviser and Director of Teacher Performance and Development. Now, more than three decades after stepping into my first classroom, I'm an Education Consultant running my own business – **Powerful Partnerships**.

In 2011, I completed a Master of Educational Leadership, focusing my research on building the capacity of others. Through that study, I discovered the potential of coaching and mentoring. I came to believe – and still do – that when we get coaching and mentoring right, we unlock transformative growth for educators and the students they serve.

Since starting Powerful Partnerships, I've worked extensively in coaching roles with individuals, schools and education systems. Students remain at the heart of all I do. I cherish every opportunity to support educators and leaders in their professional journeys and I look forward to continuing this important work for many years to come.

To find out more about Jodie Davey and the courses she offers through Powerful Partnerships, visit her website

https://www.powerfulpartnerships.com.au/

or contact Jodie directly at
jodie@powerfulpartnerships.com.au

ABOUT THIS BOOK

This book is designed to support school leaders, teachers and support staff in developing or refining coaching and mentoring practices that are not only clear and meaningful but also deeply sustainable over time. In an ever-evolving educational landscape, the need for intentional, reflective professional learning has never been more critical.

Whether you are at the very beginning of your journey into coaching and mentoring, or whether you are looking to re-energise and enhance an established approach, this book provides a comprehensive and practical guide tailored to your context.

Through a blend of evidence-informed strategies, reflective prompts and step-by-step guidance, it encourages thoughtful engagement with the principles and practices that underpin effective professional support. Each chapter is designed to spark conversation, inspire collaboration and empower educators to create a culture where learning is continuous, capacity is built collectively and growth is shared across the whole school community.

Above all, this book emphasises sustainability – ensuring that coaching and mentoring are not seen as one-off initiatives or isolated responsibilities, but as embedded, dynamic elements of everyday professional life. By fostering an environment where trust, curiosity and feedback are the norm, you can help to create a thriving culture of development that benefits all staff and, ultimately, all students.

CONTENTS

Part A –
Foundations

CHAPTER 1

Introduction

Welcome to *Coaching and Mentoring: Keeping it Simple.*

At the heart of this work is the simple but powerful idea that every educator deserves the opportunity to grow, and that growth flourishes in an environment of trust, support and collaboration. When implemented well, coaching and mentoring become more than just programs – they become part of the fabric of how a school operates, learns, and improves.

Why Coaching and Mentoring Matter

Let's start with the most important reason to invest time and effort into coaching and mentoring: because it improves teaching and, therefore, student outcomes.

Research consistently tells us that the single most important in-school factor that influences student achievement is the quality of teaching. Great teaching doesn't happen by accident. It requires deliberate practice, thoughtful reflection and ongoing support. Coaching and mentoring provide the structures and relationships that allow teachers to experiment, reflect, receive feedback and continue to evolve in their practice.

However, the impact of coaching and mentoring is only as strong as the culture in which they are embedded. In schools where these practices are misunderstood, poorly implemented or seen as a form of performance management, they can do more harm than good.

That's why this book begins with an essential message:

Coaching and mentoring are not tools for appraisal.

If coaching and mentoring are used – or even perceived – as mechanisms for evaluation or accountability, they lose their most powerful potential: to help teachers grow through vulnerability, experimentation and honest reflection. When the fear of judgement is present, teachers are less likely to take risks, admit uncertainty or seek help. As a result, learning stalls.

Instead, coaching and mentoring should provide safe, supportive spaces where educators feel free to:

- try new teaching strategies – even if they don't work at first
- talk openly about challenges without fear of judgement
- receive feedback that is constructive, not evaluative
- set their own professional goals, with guidance
- build a shared language of teaching and learning across the school.

Clarifying Purpose: Your 'Why'

Before any structure, model or framework is adopted, you need to take a step back and ask the following questions:

- Why are we doing this?
- What is the purpose of coaching and mentoring in our school?
- What do we hope it will achieve – not just for our staff, but ultimately for our students?

Every school will have a slightly different answer depending on its context. Some common goals might include:

- supporting early career teachers to build confidence and competence
- creating consistency of practice across classrooms or year levels
- embedding whole-school instructional strategies
- improving retention by helping teachers feel supported and valued
- providing professional growth pathways for experienced teachers
- promoting reflective practice and continuous improvement
- building leadership capacity across the school.

All of these are valid reasons, but without a clearly articulated purpose, even well-intentioned efforts can become disconnected or ineffective. Worse, they can be misinterpreted as performance monitoring, particularly if coaching conversations are linked to formal observations, data tracking or teacher evaluations.

The Risk of Confusing Coaching with Appraisal

One of the biggest challenges in implementing coaching and mentoring is separating them from the formal appraisal process. While leadership teams understandably need to monitor the quality of teaching and ensure standards are met, those functions must be kept separate from growth-focused professional conversations.

If a teacher suspects that their coaching session might be reported to a line manager or used in an appraisal meeting, their openness will be compromised. The same is true if the coach or mentor is also the person responsible for evaluating their performance. The tension this creates often leads to guarded conversations, minimal risk-taking and a focus on compliance rather than growth.

Coaching and mentoring should be seen as developmental, not judgemental.

Of course, leadership teams still need to oversee staff performance. Accountability still matters, but that must be addressed through separate channels. Coaching and mentoring, when kept free from appraisal, allow teachers to focus on their learning without fear.

Building a Culture for Growth

At their best, coaching and mentoring contribute to a whole-school culture of professional learning. This is a culture where:

- teachers regularly reflect on their practice
- professional conversations are part of everyday life
- feedback is welcomed and acted upon

- staff feel supported, not scrutinised
- everyone, from beginning teachers to experienced leaders, sees themself as a learner.

Developing this kind of culture takes time, consistency and clear communication. It also takes leadership – both from formal leaders and from those who coach or mentor their peers. Throughout this book, you'll find strategies to help build and maintain a strong foundation for growth.

Your First Task: Define and Discuss Your 'Why'

Before moving into frameworks, models or tools, your first priority is to define your purpose. Use the following questions as a starting point for discussion with your team.

- What are we aiming to achieve through coaching and mentoring?
- Why is this important for our staff and students?
- What practices are currently in place in our school?
- How do staff feel about these practices?
- Do they believe coaching or mentoring is being used for appraisal?
- How do staff respond to feedback – are they open or hesitant?
- What conditions would help build trust in these processes?
- What kind of culture do we want to build in our school?

These questions will spark honest, open dialogue, and they'll bring together diverse voices. The more inclusive the conversation, the more ownership and trust you'll build from the outset.

This book is about keeping things simple, but powerful. The goal isn't to implement a complex model or a checklist of best practices. It's to build something real, something that fits your context and something that helps every teacher become the best educator they can be for the students who depend on them.

Let's begin.

CHAPTER 2

What is Coaching and Mentoring?

Coaching and mentoring are terms that are often used together – sometimes even interchangeably – in conversations about professional learning. However, while they may serve related purposes and sometimes overlap in practice, **they are not the same**. Each has its own distinct focus, approach and skill set, and each plays a critical role at different points in a teacher's professional learning journey.

The Four Stages of Competence

To help us explore the unique characteristics of coaching and mentoring, we can turn to the Four Stages of Competence – a well-established model of adult learning that describes how individuals progress from ignorance to mastery. This model provides a powerful lens through which we can understand when and how different types of support are most effective.

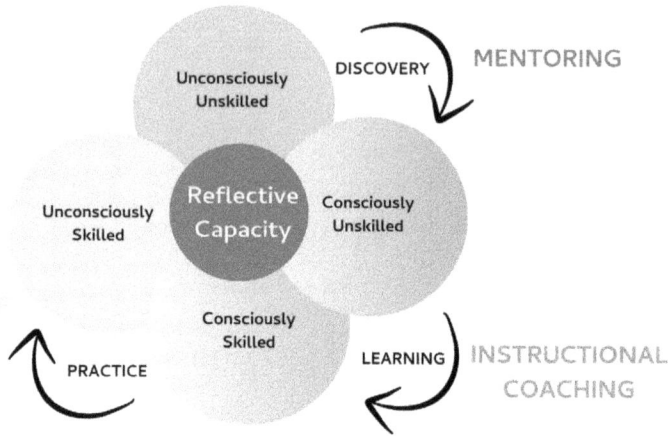

This framework, which first appeared in the 1960s and was later made popular by Martin M. Broadwell in a 1969 article titled *The Four Levels of Teaching*, outlines a progression that all learners pass through as they develop a new skill or area of knowledge.

The four stages are:

1. Unconsciously incompetent (unconsciously unskilled)

2. Consciously incompetent (consciously unskilled)

3. Consciously competent (consciously skilled)

4. Unconsciously competent (unconsciously skilled)

Let's take a look at each stage in more detail, along with the type of coach or mentor needed.

Unconsciously Incompetent

At this stage, the learner is unaware of their lack of knowledge or skill. They don't know what they don't know. As a result, they may not yet see the value in learning the new skill or concept, and they might even resist feedback or support because they don't recognise that it applies to them.

This is a common starting point for:

- pre-service teachers
- graduate and early career teachers
- staff entering new teaching contexts (e.g. switching year levels or curriculum areas).

Enter the Mentor

The mentor's role here is pivotal. They must gently guide the learner toward discovering what they don't yet know. This is a process of **discovery** – it requires insight, patience and a non-judgemental approach.

Mentors create safe environments for exploratory conversations and provide feedback that is framed as curiosity rather than criticism. They might ask questions like:

- What do you notice about how students responded to that approach?
- Have you seen how others are managing that aspect?
- What might be another way to think about that strategy?

Mentoring at this stage is less about fixing and more about **revealing**. The goal is to move the learner from unconscious to conscious recognition of their learning needs.

Consciously Incompetent

At this stage, the learner is aware of their gaps. They understand that they lack a particular skill or piece of knowledge and begin to see the value in addressing that gap. This can be a vulnerable time – frustration or self-doubt may emerge – but it's also a rich opportunity for growth.

This is where true **learning** begins.

Enter the Instructional Coach

Once the learner is motivated and ready, the instructional coach provides **structured teaching** of the new skill or concept. This could include:

- modelling the strategy
- breaking the task into steps
- co-planning lessons
- co-teaching or observing and giving feedback
- using data to inform practice.

The coach helps the teacher focus on **how** to implement a strategy effectively and **why** it works. They scaffold learning, help problem-solve and check for understanding.

It's important to note:

Instructional coaching is most effective only after mentoring has helped the learner realise they are ready.

Trying to teach a strategy to someone who doesn't yet see the need for it is often met with resistance or confusion. Mentoring paves the way for coaching to succeed.

Consciously Competent

The learner can now perform the skill or strategy, but it still requires concentration and effort. They may be following a script or checklist. Mistakes are still common, but they're learning from them. The learner is no longer asking, "What do I need to do?"

but rather, "Am I doing this right?" or "How can I do it better?"

Enter the Peer Coach

Peer coaches offer **encouragement, affirmation and collaborative reflection**. Their primary role is not to correct or instruct, but to provide a sounding board and support system as the learner consolidates their practice.

Peer coaching is powerful because it:

- normalises professional dialogue
- reduces isolation
- promotes a growth mindset
- encourages persistence through the messy middle of learning.

Think of the peer coach as a **cheerleader and thinking partner**. They might say:

- That part really worked; what do you think made the difference?
- You handled that student's response really smoothly!
- It's great to see how far you've come since last term.

In this stage, the learner needs **practice**, **patience** and **encouragement**. The peer coach creates the space for all three.

Unconsciously Competent

Now, the learner has embedded the skill so deeply that it has become second nature. They no longer have to think step-by-step – it flows naturally. They may begin to innovate, adapt or combine the skill with others in new ways. They can multitask while using it, and they may not even realise how proficient they've become.

At this stage, the learner may:

- serve as a model for others
- mentor peers or new staff
- reflect more deeply on subtleties of their practice
- shift their focus to more complex skills.

Enter Self-Reflection and Leadership

Although external support is less critical here, the reflective mindset continues to drive growth. The teacher may now be positioned to **mentor or coach others**, contribute to professional learning communities or engage in leadership roles that support whole-school improvement.

The Thread That Connects All Four Stages: Reflection

Across every stage, **self-reflection** is essential. It acts as a bridge from one stage to the next and ensures learning is internalised rather than performed on the surface.

Schools that prioritise reflective practice:

- create space for honest dialogue
- encourage professional journalling or coaching conversations
- celebrate vulnerability and risk-taking
- shift the culture from 'evaluation' to 'evolution'.

Educators who are reflective:

- learn more deeply and retain learning longer
- become more adaptive and innovative

- are more likely to take ownership of their professional growth.

The following table offers a summary of the Four Stages of Competence.

Stage of Competence	Learning Mindset	Primary Support Role	Focus of Support
1. Unconsciously Unskilled	Discovery and awareness	**Mentor**	Reveal gaps and spark motivation
2. Consciously Unskilled	Motivation and instruction	**Instructional Coach**	Teach and model the new skill
3. Consciously Skilled	Application and practice	**Peer Coach**	Encourage and sustain effort
4. Unconsciously Skilled	Mastery and transfer	**Self-Reflection / Leader**	Reflect, share and lead others

Coaching and Mentoring: The Difference

Understanding the difference between coaching and mentoring is not about creating rigid roles. Instead, it's about understanding the **needs of the learner** and matching them with the right type of support at the right time. When schools do this well, they create environments where teachers feel safe, supported and professionally nourished.

- **Mentoring** helps teachers discover what they need.
- **Instructional Coaching** helps teachers learn how to do it.
- **Peer Coaching** helps teachers refine and own it.

- **Reflection** turns all of it into lasting growth.

When these elements work in harmony, schools become vibrant places of adult learning – and students benefit from classrooms led by reflective, skilled and empowered educators.

CHAPTER 3

What Makes an Effective Coach or Mentor?

As we deepen our understanding of the distinct roles that coaches and mentors play in the development of teachers, it becomes increasingly important to ensure that the right individuals are selected and supported in these roles. While both positions require specific attributes and training, the role of a mentor is particularly critical for teachers in the early stages of their careers, or for those navigating a significant professional transition.

This chapter will address the qualities of effective mentoring, along with what is needed for effective coaching.

Effective Mentors

Mentoring serves as a foundational support system for teachers who are:

- new to the profession (pre-service, graduate or early-career teachers)
- new to a school or system
- new to a year level, subject or role

- not new to teaching but returning after a (significant) break.

These educators often face unfamiliar contexts and uncharted challenges. The common theme among these groups is that they are in the stage of **unconsciously unskilled** – that is, they 'don't know what they don't know'. In these cases, mentoring helps shine a light on areas that may be overlooked and then supports educators in building the awareness, skills and confidence they need to thrive.

The Purpose of Mentoring

The primary role of a mentor is to guide, support and challenge the mentee's professional growth. This goes beyond offering assistance and involves:

- identifying learning gaps
- encouraging reflection
- offering constructive feedback
- prioritising developmental goals
- creating opportunities for skill-building.

Mentors should act as **guides**, helping mentees navigate the profession. They should also act as **role models**, demonstrating best practices in pedagogy, leadership and professional behaviour.

Characteristics of Effective Mentors

An effective mentor possesses a blend of personal attributes and professional expertise. Ideal mentors are:

- patient and empathetic – they understand that learning is a process and growth takes time

- experienced and knowledgeable – they have a strong foundation in teaching practice, curriculum knowledge and school culture
- non-judgemental and welcoming – they create a safe environment where mentees feel comfortable being honest about their struggles
- trust builders – they prioritise developing a genuine, respectful relationship
- proactive communicators – they do not wait for the mentee to ask for help; instead, they actively check in, provide guidance and ensure consistent interaction
- excellent listeners and questioners – they use open-ended questions to prompt deeper thinking and reflection
- skilled feedback providers – they give feedback that is timely, evidence-based and focused on growth.

Selecting the Right Mentors

The success of a mentoring program depends largely on who is chosen to be the mentor. Selecting mentors purely based on logistical convenience – such as being on the same year level teaching team, or in the same staffroom or faculty – can lead to superficial, or purely operational relationships. While such arrangements may help with day-to-day queries, they do not always provide the professional depth and intentional development that mentoring requires.

Instead, it is important that schools prioritise mentors who have a genuine desire to help others grow. Mentors must see the role as a privilege and a responsibility, not just an administrative duty. Passion, curiosity and a growth mindset are essential traits.

The most effective mentors often describe mentoring as a way to give back to the profession, and as a means of self-reflection and learning.

Strategic Mentoring: Prioritising What Matters Most

Mentors play a key role in helping mentees prioritise their learning. For example, a common challenge for early-career teachers is determining where to focus their energy. Without guidance, a teacher may choose to spend extensive time on superficial aspects (e.g. classroom décor or displays), rather than foundational ones (e.g. routines, behaviour management and student engagement strategies).

Mentors must draw on their experience to guide these decisions. For example, a mentor might help the mentee understand that establishing strong classroom routines and behaviour expectations in the first few weeks will have a more lasting impact than the layout of a classroom display. In this sense, mentors provide a strategic lens, helping the mentee invest in 'big wins' first.

Mentor Knowledge and Expertise

To be truly effective, mentors need more than goodwill. They require a solid understanding of:

- the teacher registration process, including expectations for evidence collection, observations and portfolio preparation
- relevant professional frameworks, such as the Australian Institute for Teachers and School Leaders (AITSL)'s Australian Professional Standards for Teachers (APST) and local jurisdiction requirements
- classroom management techniques, from establishing

routines to handling challenging behaviours

- contemporary pedagogical approaches, including differentiation, formative assessment and feedback strategies
- assessment and reporting strategies, including understanding how to design, deliver and interpret assessments in line with curriculum requirements.

Mentors should also be familiar with relevant digital tools, policies and professional learning communities so they can direct mentees to appropriate resources.

Commitment and Continuity in Mentoring

Unlike coaching, which can be short-term or goal-specific, mentoring is a sustained commitment. It is not about quick fixes, but about deep, transformative growth over time. Ideally, a mentoring relationship should last twelve to twenty-four months, providing the mentee with a stable source of guidance through their early years of teaching.

Regular contact is essential, and it is important for mentors to:

- schedule regular meetings
- engage in ongoing dialogue with their mentee
- observe classroom practice and offer feedback
- support the creation and review of professional goals
- provide emotional encouragement during challenging times.

Mentors as Advocates for the Profession

Lastly, and perhaps most importantly, it is essential that mentors serve as ambassadors for teaching. With increasing pressures, workload concerns and negative public narratives, the morale of early-career teachers can be fragile. Mentors play a vital role in nurturing optimism, fostering resilience and reinforcing the value of the profession.

It is important that mentors not only remind their mentees of the impact they will have on young lives, but also to celebrate small victories and promote a positive and hopeful vision of what it means to be an educator. In doing so, mentors contribute to the development of individual teachers, as well as to the long-term sustainability of the profession.

Effective Coaches

When developing or evaluating a coaching model in education, it's essential to understand the specific attributes that make a coach effective. While there are similarities between coaches and mentors – such as offering guidance, support and professional development – coaching has distinct characteristics. Effective coaching requires a set of refined interpersonal and professional skills that foster trust, reflection and growth in the individuals being coached.

Establishing and Maintaining Trust

At the heart of every successful coaching relationship lies trust. Without trust, meaningful dialogue and genuine progress are almost impossible. Teachers must feel secure enough to share challenges, admit uncertainties and explore new approaches to their practice. This sense of psychological safety doesn't occur automatically – it must be carefully cultivated by the coach from the outset.

Trust is built through:

- reliability – following through on commitments and being consistently supportive
- integrity – demonstrating honesty, fairness and a non-judgemental attitude
- confidentiality – upholding the private nature of coaching conversations.

The last point, in particular, is crucial. Any perceived link between coaching and formal appraisal can severely limit the openness and success of the relationship.

Coaches must continually reassure teachers that what is shared in coaching sessions will not be used for evaluative purposes. This not only reduces fear of failure but also encourages experimentation and reflective practice.

Being Present and Actively Listening

Effective coaches bring their full presence to every interaction. Being 'present' means more than just being physically in the room; it requires undivided attention, emotional awareness and cognitive focus.

Active listening involves:

- tuning in to verbal and non-verbal cues
- avoiding distractions
- limiting the tendency towards multitasking
- demonstrating genuine interest in the teacher's thoughts and experiences.

Importantly, it is essential that coaches resist the impulse to jump to solutions or advice-giving. The role of the coach is not to fix but to facilitate the teacher's thinking process. By fully engaging in dialogue, the coach creates a space where the teacher feels heard, valued and empowered to explore their own insights.

Empathy and Clarification

Empathy is a critical coaching skill that allows coaches to connect on a human level. Empathetic coaches can see things from the teacher's perspective and respond with understanding rather than judgement. This emotional attunement builds rapport and increases the coachee's comfort in expressing themselves honestly.

In addition to empathy, effective coaches excel in clarification – the ability to unpack what is being said, probe beneath the surface and ensure mutual understanding. This might involve paraphrasing, summarising or asking for elaboration.

These skills ensure that:

- misunderstandings are minimised
- coaching sessions stay focused on meaningful, relevant goals
- the teacher feels validated and supported, yet also gently challenged when necessary.

Delivering Feedback and Enabling Action

An essential part of coaching is the ability to provide constructive, evidence-informed feedback in a way that promotes growth rather than defensiveness. Feedback should be:

- specific and actionable
- grounded in observable behaviour or evidence

- delivered in a manner that invites reflection, not resistance.

However, giving feedback is only half of the equation. Effective coaches also help teachers to make sense of the feedback and take tangible steps toward improvement. This may include setting goals, developing action plans or modelling techniques. The ultimate aim is not just to share insights, but to facilitate meaningful change in practice.

Mastering the Art of Questioning

Perhaps the most powerful skill in a coach's toolkit is the ability to ask the right questions.

Coaching is inherently a collaborative, inquiry-driven process. The best coaches are expert questioners who use thoughtful, open-ended questions to spark reflection, challenge assumptions and guide self-discovery. Two effective questioning frameworks can be found in Chapter 4 of this book.

Effective coaching questions:

- invite deep thinking (e.g. What do you notice about how students responded to that strategy?)
- encourage ownership (e.g. What do you think you might try next time?)
- promote self-efficacy (e.g. What strengths can you build on here?).

Rather than providing solutions, powerful questions help teachers unlock their own ideas, insights, and strategies for improvement. This approach fosters autonomy, confidence, and professional agency.

In Summary

Effective mentoring requires intentional selection, sustained commitment and deep professional knowledge. When mentors are chosen for their skills, passion and character – not just their convenience – and when they prioritise trust, structure and inspiration, they can make a significant difference in the development of early-career and transitioning teachers.

The most effective coaches combine emotional intelligence with professional expertise to create a partnership where trust, inquiry and development can flourish. These coaches maintain confidentiality, demonstrate engagement and empathy, ask insightful questions and provide constructive feedback as they guide actionable steps.

While coaches and mentors may share some overlapping responsibilities, the coaching relationship is uniquely non-directive, confidential and reflective. The focus is on growth through guided dialogue, whereas a mentor's focus is on advice or instruction.

Whether coaching or mentoring, it is essential that we build a culture that uplifts educators, makes a significant impact on teaching practice and learning outcomes, and ultimately strengthens schools from within.

CHAPTER 4

Questioning Frameworks

Mentoring and coaching are dynamic, human-centered processes. Attempting to script these conversations can feel rigid, impersonal and even counterproductive. While it might be tempting to rely on a pre-written list of questions or talking points, real growth and meaningful dialogue occur when conversations are flexible, responsive and authentic.

Every mentee or coachee brings a unique context – different experiences, personalities, goals and challenges. Trying to fit these individual realities into a fixed script risks:

- suppressing genuine responses
- stifling creativity
- undermining trust and openness
- creating a power imbalance.

Instead, using a questioning framework offers structure without confinement. The framework serves as scaffolding, not a cage, guiding conversations in a meaningful direction while allowing room for organic exploration.

The remainder of this chapter will look at two frameworks in more detail – the ORID Model of Questioning, and the GROW Model of Coaching.

The ORID Model of Questioning

The Objective, Reflective, Interpretive, Decisional (ORID) Model of Questioning was first developed by Joseph Matthews, a US Army chaplain, in the aftermath of World War II. He witnessed firsthand the emotional and psychological burden carried by returning soldiers and civilians. Matthews created this model to help people process complex experiences, especially trauma, through structured reflection.

So, how is a structure that was developed for returned soldiers useful in the educational context?

ORID allows for the promotion of deep reflection, provides structure and clarity, assists in building trust and psychological safety and leads to actionable outcomes.

Rather than telling teachers what to do, mentors using ORID guide teachers to reach their own conclusions. This promotes agency, confidence and professional growth.

By guiding conversations through ORID, mentors help teachers think critically, learn from experience and grow professionally – which is the heart of effective mentoring.

Structure of ORID

Type	Purpose	Examples
O – Objective	Focus on what can be observed, measured or proven. No opinions or interpretations allowed here. It's about establishing a shared reality.	"What did you observe in your class this week?" "What strategies are you currently using?" "What does the student data indicate?"
R – Reflective	Tap into the learner's emotions, preferences and inner responses to their experiences. This builds emotional engagement and personal insight.	"What's working well for you right now?" "What's been frustrating?" "What are you most proud of?"
I – Interpretive	Help the mentee analyse and make meaning from the facts and feelings. This stage explores values, motivations and implications.	"Why do you think that strategy is effective?" "What does that outcome mean for your students?" "Why do you think this is happening?"
D – Decisional	Transition into goal setting and planning. Here, the conversation becomes action-oriented.	"What steps will you take next?" "How can I support you in this goal?" "When will you try this new strategy?"

Why ROID May Work Better in Mentoring

In mentoring, we often flip the Objective (O) and Reflective (R) stages – creating the ROID model – especially with novice teachers. The Objective line of questioning can feel overwhelming. For example, if we ask a beginning teacher an objective question such as "What does your data say about student engagement?", they may not feel confident in their ability to interpret, or even collect, data yet. Therefore, starting with reflective questions can be more effective.

Try starting with questions like:

- "What's brought you joy in the classroom lately?"
- "What small wins have you noticed?"
- "What are you unsure about?"

Taking this approach – the ROID variation of Reflective → Objective → Interpretive → Decisional – creates a safer, more trusting environment. Reflective questions invite the mentee to open up emotionally, making the subsequent stages (Objective, Interpretive, Decisional) more productive and relevant.

The GROW Model of Coaching

The Goal, Reality, Options, Will (GROW) Model of Coaching was developed in the 1980s by performance and executive coaches including Sir John Whitmore, Graham Alexander and Alan Fine. The model became popular in business and leadership development and has since been widely adopted in areas like education, sport and life coaching.

Unlike ORID (ROID), the GROW model is designed for goal-driven conversations where the coachee already has some degree of awareness or clarity about what they want to achieve.

Structure of GROW

Type	Purpose	Examples
G – Goal	Clarify the coachee's aspirations and long-term aims. This stage sets the direction and provides motivation.	"What would success look like for you?" "What's the ideal outcome for you?" "Why is this important to you?"
R – Reality	Examine the current situation, strengths and challenges. Ground the conversation in truth.	"What's happening now?" "What's working well already?" "What are the challenges you're facing?"
O – Options	Brainstorm multiple strategies without judgement. The more creative and open-ended, the better.	"What are some ways you could move forward?" "What else could you try?" "If anything were possible, what would you do?"
W – Will	Solidify commitment, plan specific next steps and anticipate obstacles. This stage transforms ideas into actions.	"What will you do next, and when?" "What might get in your way?" "How will you keep yourself accountable?"

Let's look at each of the components in a little more detail, in the context of education, with a scenario and some specific questions using the GROW structure.

Scenario:
A Year 6 teacher is struggling to keep students engaged during mathematics lessons. Despite thorough lesson planning, students seem distracted, and the teacher feels frustrated and unsure how to increase participation and motivation.

Goal Setting: Visualise and Inspire

This stage isn't just about identifying a goal – it's about emotionally connecting the coachee to the goal. Visualisation and emotive language help deepen commitment.

Ask:

- What would you like to achieve with your maths lessons over the next few weeks?
- If this lesson were going exactly how you wanted, what would it look like?
- What would success in student engagement mean to you?

Reality: Focus on Strengths

In this stage, instead of fixating on what's wrong, help the coachee to focus on what's going right by asking questions such as:

- What's currently happening during your maths lessons that pleases you?
- How do your students typically respond during these activities?
- What have you already tried to do to improve engagement?
- How do you feel at the end of a typical maths lesson?

Options: Encourage Wild Thinking

In this stage, we want to generate ideas. Encourage the coachee to break free from their internal critic. Eliminate the "Yeah but…"

Use prompts like:

- What strategies have you seen or heard of that could work in this context?

- What might happen if you incorporated more hands-on activities or group work?

- What could you try that's different?

- Who could you observe or collaborate with to get new ideas?

Will: Create an Action Plan
This is the stage where commitment happens.

Be specific:

- Which option feels most doable right now?

- What will you do before our next coaching conversation?

- What might get in the way of implementing this plan, and how will you handle that?

- How will you measure whether your strategy is working?

Using Questioning Frameworks Effectively

It's all good to have these frameworks, but how do you use them effectively? Here are a few tips and tricks (that we know work).

- Record conversations: this allows both coach and coachee, or the mentor and mentee to reflect later and build on previous insights.

- Name and affirm strengths: positivity fuels progress.

- Avoid judgement: stay curious, not critical.

- Help build a toolkit: encourage the development of a personal bank of resources, strategies and support networks.

- Stay flexible: use frameworks as guides, not scripts. Be willing to veer off-track when the conversation requires it.

Choosing the Right Framework

How do you know which framework to choose? Here's a quick guide to get you started.

Scenario	Best-Suited Framework	Why?
A novice teacher unsure where to begin	ROID (Mentoring)	It encourages reflection rather than needing the correct answer. It helps build a relationship between mentee and mentor. It helps identify relevant areas to work on together.
An experienced professional looking to solve a specific challenge	GROW (Coaching)	The experienced teacher is more likely able to identify key areas for growth themselves and set meaningful goals without the coach needing to help them reflect on their practice.
Building trust in early-stage conversations	Start with Reflective (ROID)	Far less threatening. Demonstrates that the coach actually cares about the coachee and what they want to work on.
Driving results and accountability	Use Will (GROW) phase effectively	This stage takes the conversation from 'just a chat' to actionable steps for improvement.

In Summary

Whether you're mentoring a new teacher or coaching a seasoned professional, great conversations begin with great questions. Frameworks like ROID and GROW help you:

- stay focused yet flexible
- move from insight to action
- foster trust and ownership.

Rather than using these models to control the conversation, use them to cultivate curiosity, empower others and guide growth – all while keeping the human connection front and centre.

Part B –
Mentoring

CHAPTER 5

Mentoring Early Career Teachers:
A Whole School Approach

O ver the course of my decades in schools, I have been privileged to witness many extraordinary initiatives driven by passionate, committed educators. These teachers pour their time and energy, and often their personal resources, into projects they believe in; projects that add tremendous value to the school community. From sustainability champions transforming disused corners into vibrant vegetable gardens, to literacy lovers turning Book Week into a magical festival of imagination and storytelling, these teachers don't just meet expectations, they redefine them.

I once worked with a librarian whose entire year seemed to orbit around Book Week. Her dedication was infectious. She arranged for authors to visit, coordinated book-themed dress-up parades, decorated the library like a wonderland and ensured every single detail – from bookmarks to banners – was considered. One year, I drove to school dressed in a full 'Bananas in Pyjamas' costume, complete with a towering banana head that forced me to tilt awkwardly to the left as I navigated traffic.

(Safety questionable, enthusiasm undeniable).

The event was always a huge success. Families lined the walkways; students beamed with pride and teachers embraced the fun. This teacher-librarian's passion had a ripple effect that united the school. You could see her smile from across the yard, stretching from ear to ear.

Similarly, every school has that one teacher who becomes the 'environmental warrior'. They care deeply about our planet and bring that passion into the school space. They start worm farms, build frog ponds, plant veggie patches and teach students about water conservation. They don't just talk sustainability, they live it. Their efforts create real impact and nurture a school-wide awareness of our shared responsibility to care for the environment.

These projects, while inspirational, often hinge on a single person. In the same way, mentoring programs for early career teachers are often driven by a single teacher or executive. And herein lies the challenge.

The Problem with 'Projects'

While these individuals deserve to be celebrated for their drive and commitment, they often shoulder the bulk of the responsibility alone. And when they move on – whether for a promotion, long service leave or simply a new chapter – the project often collapses. The Book Week festival becomes a quiet classroom story time. The once-lush garden shrivels and is handed over to the groundskeeper.

This isn't always a problem. Schools naturally shift focus from year to year depending on staffing and interests. Some ebb and flow is healthy.

---

*But this cannot be the case for the
mentoring of Early Career Teachers (ECTs).*

While Book Week and vegetable patches enrich school life, mentoring ECTs is about the long-term sustainability of our profession. It's about ensuring our newest teachers thrive, grow, and feel supported as they begin one of the most complex and rewarding careers.

And yet, in too many schools, mentoring suffers the same fate as the 'passion project'. A dedicated leader does wonderful work, supports and uplifts new staff, and builds strong mentoring relationships – but when they leave, the support falls away. There is no structure in place. No handover. No cultural expectation that mentoring is **everyone's** responsibility.

This is why we must move toward a **whole school approach** to mentoring.

Why a Whole School Approach Matters

To ensure mentoring is not left to chance, schools must intentionally embed it into their systems, culture and values. This means building mentoring into the fabric of how we operate so it continues regardless of individual leadership. Just like we plan for curriculum, behaviour management and student wellbeing, we must plan for how we support and develop our newest staff members.

Mentoring should not rely on goodwill alone. It should be a structured, supported and visible process that is embraced by the whole community.

When mentoring is systemic, it:

- provides consistency and continuity year after year
- encourages collaboration and shared responsibility
- builds leadership capacity across the staff
- supports teacher wellbeing and retention
- fosters a professional learning culture.

The Three Pillars

Developing and retaining high-quality educators begins with a deep commitment to support, especially for early career teachers. To build this strong foundation, three key areas require careful and consistent attention. Known as the 'three pillars', these are:

- school systems and culture
- teaching and learning
- relationships.

Each of these pillars plays a critical role in ensuring that early career teachers are not only welcomed into the school community but are also supported in thriving professionally and personally.

The following section will look at each of the three pillars in more detail.

School Systems and Culture

The systems and culture are among the first experiences that shape a new teacher's impression of their workplace. Clear structures, supportive routines and inclusive values create a setting in which new teachers can find their place.

Induction: Beyond a One-Off Event

Many schools and systems have a formal induction program, often held in Week 0 or prior to the start of the year. While this is valuable, it is often content-heavy, fast-paced and overwhelming. A more strategic and human-centred approach involves spacing out the information and focusing on connection and clarity.

Key Considerations for Effective Induction

There are a number of points to consider if an induction is to be practical and effective for ECTs.

- **When and how to share information**

  Overloading new teachers with all policies, procedures, codes, systems and schedules at once can result in cognitive overload. Instead, prioritise what is essential for Week 1 and phase in additional information during Term 1 and beyond.

- **How to balance information with relationships**

  Make space during induction to share stories, values and school culture. Invite teachers to reflect on why they chose education and what excites them about their role. Build time for personal connection – not just professional orientation.

- **Prepare ECTs for long-term success rather than short-term survival**

  The goal is not to front-load every detail but to equip new teachers to know where to find help and who to go to when challenges arise.

Choose the Right Mentors

The right mentor makes all the difference. Assigned mentors should embody the school's values and demonstrate a genuine desire to support others. Avoid assigning mentors based on availability or location alone – this is not just a role; it's a relationship.

Characteristics of effective mentors include:

- demonstrating positivity, patience and empathy
- being skilled in pedagogy and school systems
- are willing to invest time
- are open to learning as well as teaching
- an ability to provide feedback constructively.

Mentors need support too. Consider offering:

- professional learning for mentors on coaching and mentoring strategies
- regular mentor forums for sharing experiences and troubleshooting challenges
- recognition and appreciation for the critical role mentors play.

Mentor Involvement from Day One

Once mentors are assigned, invite them to participate in the induction process, not just in formal sessions but in informal, relationship-building moments. A shared morning tea or lunch is a simple but powerful act.

Reflection Questions for Leadership Teams

Reflection is essential for leadership teams to ensure any

induction are meeting their goals. Ask questions like:

- Are we focusing more on content than connection?
- Do new teachers leave induction feeling supported or overwhelmed?
- Could we seek feedback from previous inductees to improve future processes?

Practical Systems to Sustain Mentorship

Mentoring programs don't just happen, they are part of a coordinated system. To help sustain the mentoring programs, schools can implement the following actions:

- **Scheduled Meetings**

  Organise regular check-ins (weekly or fortnightly) between mentors and mentees – and put them on the calendar. If they're not on the calendar, they risk being sidelined by the busyness of school life.

- **Mentor-Mentee Resource Hub**

  Create a shared digital space or handbook that includes key contacts, expectations, routines, classroom setup tips, curriculum overviews and frequently asked questions.

- **Sample Term-by-Term Induction Map**

  Provide a timeline that outlines when different areas of the school will be introduced (e.g. Week 1: classroom setup and student expectations, Week 3: assessment overview, Week 5: communication with parents).

The Marigold Principle

A helpful analogy is the **Marigold and Walnut** metaphor.

Marigolds are companion plants that support growth in neigh-bouring plants, while walnuts release chemicals that inhibit growth. In schools:

- marigolds are the positive, encouraging, solution-focused staff who nurture others
- walnuts are the negative, cynical and energy-draining staff who undermine confidence.

Place early career teachers near your marigolds – both physi-cally (classroom proximity) and socially (staffroom groupings, team teaching or shared planning).

If you do an internet search for 'The Marigold Effect' (or look for it on my YouTube channel), you'll find a short video you can share with your mentors and mentees.

Teaching and Learning

At the heart of every school is its core purpose: teaching and learning. Early career teachers often arrive enthusiastic and ready to make a difference. However, without strategic support, that enthusiasm can quickly turn into fatigue and frustration.

Protecting Their Energy

Early career teachers need encouragement to **pace themselves**. While they may be eager to coach sports teams, be involved in school musicals or join any number of committees, effective classroom teaching must remain as their core business.

To help early career teachers with strategies for energy manage-ment, mentors, with the support of the leadership team, could:

- encourage a balance between work and rest

- provide permission to say no to additional commitments in the first year
- normalise that teaching improves over time, and they are not expected to master everything in their first term.

Pedagogical Support

This is where mentorship and leadership must be intentional. It's not enough to just check in emotionally, it's also important we support instructional growth.

Areas of focus may include:

- **classroom management** through helping new teachers set clear expectations and routines from day one, observing their classroom and providing timely feedback
- **curriculum and assessment** through assisting new teachers to unpack learning outcomes, understand and apply backwards mapping, and align assessment with standards
- **observation and modelling** through allowing early career teachers to observe skilled teachers in action, then debriefing these experiences to highlight key takeaways.
- **feedback cycles** through providing regular, formative feedback that highlights strengths and identifies one or two areas for growth at a time.

Support with Planning

Planning takes time and early career teachers often struggle to find balance between over-planning and under-preparing. Mentors can provide templates, scope-and-sequence guides and examples of unit plans to help.

Encouraging Self-Reflection

Mentors can ask reflective questions such as:

- What felt successful in that lesson?

- Where did students seem confused or disengaged?

- What might you try differently next time?

Discussions prompted by these types of questions foster metacognition and professional agency.

Navigating Parent Communication

The idea of having to communicate with parents and other caregivers often brings anxiety to early career teachers as they may lack experience or confidence.

Strategies to support early career teachers to communicate effectively with parents include:

- providing scripts or sentence starters for common conversations

- role-playing difficult conversations, such as discussing behaviour or low achievement

- encouraging early, positive contact with parents to build rapport and trust.

Relationships

Human connection is foundational to teacher success. When early career teachers feel isolated, unsupported or invisible, their likelihood of burnout increases. Strong relationships help buffer stress and build resilience.

Collegial Relationships

Good working relationships are essential for all teachers, but particularly early career teachers who often feel isolated. Strategies that support the development of collegial relationships include:

- providing a **welcoming environment** where early career teachers are introduced to staff across departments, not just their immediate team
- nurturing a positive **staffroom culture** by encouraging inclusivity in staff common areas with mentors assisting by physically inviting new staff to join them
- helping early career teachers establish support networks by identifying key go-to people for curriculum, wellbeing, administration, tech support and behaviour support.

Student Relationships

The most important relationships a teacher will have are those with their students.

The key areas that support this include:

- **getting to know students**, where the mentor can provide tools and strategies for learning names, understanding interests and recognising strengths
- **building rapport with boundaries**, where the mentor can help new teachers navigate friendly, firm relationships that maintain authority while being approachable
- **establishing behaviour management** strategies so early career teachers can develop consistent responses,

understand school-wide expectations and use restorative practices effectively when needed.

Wellbeing and Workload

Teaching is emotionally and intellectually demanding. Early career teachers, who may be perfectionists or people-pleasers, need active encouragement to:

- set boundaries around their workday
- recognise the value of rest and recovery
- seek support when struggling
- know that mistakes are part of the journey.

Mentors and leaders must monitor teachers for early signs of stress, burnout or disengagement. Proactive check-ins, affirmation and reassurance go a long way.

Creating a Culture Where Teachers Thrive

When schools invest in their new teachers – not just at induction but consistently throughout their first few years – they are building a sustainable, supportive and high-impact educational culture.

A strong induction process, combined with a commitment to instructional mentorship and a focus on relationship-building lay the foundation for a thriving school.

Let us be intentional. Let us be relational. Let us create the kind of school where all teachers feel they belong, matter and can grow.

CHAPTER 6

Yearly Plan

This chapter contains a year-long timeline of induction, mentorship and professional growth. It is an example only and you are encouraged to use this to guide the development of a mentoring framework that suits your school.

Welcome, Orientation and Induction

When: pre-term (week 0)

Focus: connection, clarity and confidence

Goals:

- Make new teachers feel welcomed and valued.
- Introduce only essential systems and contacts.
- Begin relationship-building with mentors and teams.

Week	Focus	Details	Responsibility
Week before Term 1	Welcome email/ call	Welcome message with logistics, mentor info	Deputy Principal or Team Leader
Week 0	Induction day(s)	Tour, introductions, wellbeing focus, essential policies only	School Leadership Team
Week 0	Mentor meet and greet	Informal lunch, expectations shared	Mentors
Week 0	Tech and tools	Laptop setup, access to Drive, brief intro to key systems	IT / Admin
Week 0	Classroom setup support	Provide time and assistance setting up classroom	Year Level Coordinator / Mentor

Foundations and Relationships

When: Term 1

Focus: routines, pedagogy, support networks

Goals:

- Establish strong classroom routines.
- Build relationships with students and staff.
- Introduce instructional planning and assessment tools.

Week	Focus	Details	Responsibility
Week 1	Classroom routines check-in	Mentor observation and feedback	Mentor
Week 2	Resource orientation	Guided tour of curriculum documents, shared Drives, units of work	Mentor / Curriculum Leader
Week 3	Planning support	Joint planning meeting, tips on balancing workload	Mentor
Week 4	Observation 1	ECT observes experienced teacher, reflective debrief follows	Mentor / Team Leader
Week 5	Parent communication support	Script and support for first parent email or call	Mentor
Week 6	Self-reflection session	What's working? What's not? Use a reflection tool	Mentor
Week 8	Wellbeing check-in	Informal wellbeing conversation, workload check	Mentor / Wellbeing Coordinator

Confidence and Competence

When: Term 2

Focus: assessment, feedback, classroom practice

Goals:

- Deepen pedagogical skills.

- Build confidence with classroom management and feedback.

- Begin deeper engagement with assessment and reporting.

Week*	Focus	Details	Responsibility
Week 1	Curriculum deep dive	Discuss sequencing, differentiation, learning goals	Curriculum Leader
Week 3	Observation 2	Mentor observes ECT, provides feedback on instruction	Mentor
Week 4	Parent-teacher interview prep	Role play, script support, checklist of tips	Mentor
Week 6	Assessment design	Review assessment tasks, align with outcomes	Year Level Team / Curriculum Leader
Week 7	Report writing support	Overview of processes, tone, feedback examples	Team Leader
Week 8	Reflective practice	ECT shares a learning success and a challenge	Mentor

* Note there is not an action for every week, as the need for these lessens as the beginning teacher grows.

Autonomy and Refinement

When: Term 3

Focus: independent planning, advanced relationships, targetted growth

Goals:

- Empower teachers to plan with greater independence.
- Refine classroom strategies and parent engagement.
- Develop deeper self-awareness of teaching practice.

Week	Focus	Details	Responsibility
Week 1	Goal-setting review	Check progress on professional goals	Mentor
Week 2	Advanced behaviour strategies	Discuss escalation, restorative practices, inclusion	Wellbeing Leader / Mentor
Week 4	Cross-classroom collaboration	ECT co-teaches or collaborates with peer	Team Leader
Week 5	Learning walk	Participate in short, school-wide observation round	Mentor / Leadership Team
Week 7	Mid-year reflection	Use AITSL standards or school rubric to self-assess growth	Mentor
Week 8	Wellbeing and balance	Plan for Term 4 energy management	Wellbeing Coordinator

Consolidation and Celebration

When: Term 4

Focus: celebration, reflection, future planning

Goals:

- Celebrate progress and growth.

- Consolidate learning and prepare for next year.

- Encourage future goal setting.

Week	Focus	Details	Responsibility
Week 2	Observation 3	Formal observation with full feedback	Mentor / Assistant (or Deputy) Principal
Week 4	Contribute to planning	ECT leads or co-leads planning session for the following year	Year Level Coordinator
Week 5	Mentor hando-ver notes	Mentor prepares brief profile or notes to inform future support	Mentor
Week 6	Celebration and feedback	Shared lunch, certificates, survey for program improvement	Leadership Team
Week 7	Goal setting	Set new professional growth goals	ECT / Mentor
Week 8	Exit interview (optional)	Gather final reflec-tions, feedback on induction year	Deputy or Principal

Ongoing Throughout the Year

In addition to the above weekly scheduled focus areas, there are several other meetings and check-ins that should be slotted in periodically.

Monthly:

- Mentor meetings (formal and informal)
- Classroom drop-ins and quick feedback chats

Per Term:

- One formal observation and reflective conversation
- One team-planning session focused on growth
- At least one wellbeing check-in

As Needed:

- Support with parent contact
- Classroom management advice
- Emotional support and, if needed, referral to wellbeing team

The above example framework ensures that support for early career teachers is **intentional, staged and sustainable**. By pacing support across the year and assigning clear responsibilities, schools can reduce teacher attrition, enhance job satisfaction and strengthen professional capacity.

As mentioned, please note this is just an example. While you are welcome to use any ideas from this example, I encourage you to develop a Mentoring Framework that aligns with your school and context.

Next Steps for School Leaders

When developing, implementing or reviewing a Mentoring Framework, school leaders should consider:

- **auditing** their current mentoring systems using their framework

- **mapping** who is currently involved in Early Career Teacher support and where gaps exist

- **assembling** a small working group to adapt and implement the framework in their setting

- **scheduling** regular reviews of the mentoring program to keep it dynamic

- **sharing** their vision with staff to build collective ownership and excitement.

Part C –
Coaching

CHAPTER 7

Definitions

C oaching has gained momentum in education over the last two decades, becoming an essential part of professional learning and school improvement. While there are many definitions of coaching, each one offers a slightly different lens through which we can understand its purpose and potential. There are a few that have deeply influenced my own thinking.

From Sir John Whitmore (2003):

> *Unlocking a person's potential to maximize their own performance. It's helping them to learn rather than teaching them.*

Also in 2003, from Myles Downey:

> *The art of facilitating the performance, learning and development of another.*

And lastly from Karen Wise (2010):

> *Coaching is about enabling individuals to make conscious decisions and empowering them to become leaders in their own lives.*

From these definitions, we can distil some common and powerful themes around:

- maximising performance
- helping others learn
- facilitating growth
- empowering individuals.

These elements reflect a philosophy that coaching is not about deficit or correction but about recognising and nurturing the strengths and potential already present in every educator.

Coaching is Not About Fixing

A fundamental misconception about coaching is that it is reserved for those who are underperforming or struggling. This could not be further from the truth. Coaching is not about **fixing** people. It is about guiding them to see new possibilities, empowering them to make deliberate decisions and supporting them to develop skills, reflect on their practice and continuously grow. It is a **collaborative and developmental** relationship — not a corrective or evaluative one.

The role of the coach is multi-faceted. A good coach is a:

- skilled listener
- probing questioner
- thoughtful guide
- constructive mirror
- supportive challenger
- compassionate partner in learning.

Whether coaching is **instructional**, targetting specific practices and strategies, or **peer-based**, offering collegial reflection and mutual support, the end goal is always the same: to promote deeper thinking, improved practice and better outcomes for students.

Coaching is About Trust

At the heart of every effective coaching relationship is **trust**. Without trust, coaching becomes superficial – an exercise in compliance rather than transformation. To establish and maintain trust, coaching must be completely separate from appraisal or performance management processes. Coaching is most powerful when it occurs in a safe, non-judgemental space where teachers can try new strategies, reflect openly on challenges and grow without fear of evaluation.

To be clear, coaching is not about making judgements, offering therapy, creating dependency, imposing initiatives, confirming prejudices or providing answers.

Instead, it is about asking the right questions, providing the right support and trusting the coachee to own their growth journey.

Coaching is Not Mentoring

Mentoring typically supports new teachers or those transitioning into a new role, school or context. It is often a long-term relationship, grounded in advice-giving, modelling and guidance from an experienced professional.

Coaching, on the other hand, is accessible to all staff, regardless of career stage. It is more goal-oriented and solution-focused, and it is often shorter in duration. Coaching is usually initiated when a teacher identifies a specific area of practice they want to refine or improve.

A mentor may be a steady guide throughout a teacher's first year or two of teaching, whereas a coach may come alongside for a few weeks to support the implementation of a new strategy, then step back once the teacher has developed confidence.

Instructional and Peer Coaching

When a school is rolling out a new teaching framework, introducing a program or making a shift in behaviour management approaches, **instructional coaching** becomes an especially powerful tool.

Instructional coaches:

- model effective strategies in real classrooms
- co-teach alongside educators
- observe and reflect with staff
- demonstrate approaches, then provide space and feedback for practice.

This type of coaching ensures that implementation is not left to chance. It provides staff with accessible expertise, ongoing support and real-time guidance, which significantly increases the likelihood that new initiatives will take root and flourish.

Peer coaches may also be engaged to support continued practice, help colleagues reflect and troubleshoot after the instructional coach has laid the groundwork.

The Power of Feedback in Coaching

Feedback is one of the most critical, yet most misunderstood, elements of the coaching process.

The effectiveness of feedback depends not on how well it is

delivered, but on how well it is received and used.

As George Bernard Shaw aptly put it:

The single biggest problem in communication
is the illusion that it has taken place.

This is particularly true of feedback. A well-meaning comment can easily be misunderstood – or forgotten entirely – if the conditions are not right.

When being asked to provide feedback, we should consider the following three principles to ensure what we say is effective.

- Relationship first – the stronger the coaching relationship, the more likely the feedback will land and lead to growth.

- Clarity over comfort – while giving positive feedback is often easier, sometimes the most impactful conversations come from honest, constructive insight.

- Plan the conversation – don't improvise but do consider what you observed, how it connects to the coachee's goals, and how you will begin the conversation in a way that models trust and invites reflection.

Focus on the Strategy, Not the Person

One of the most effective ways to reduce defensiveness and increase engagement in feedback conversations is to focus on **strategies** rather than **performance**. Frame your observations around what was done and how it worked, instead of making judgements about the teacher's ability.

Ask:

- What strategies were used?
- What was the intended impact?
- What actually happened?
- How might we tweak or adjust for next time?

This approach allows the conversation to remain professional, objective and forward-looking, rather than personal or evaluative.

A coaching conversation should be interactive – remember, dialogue, not monologue. If you find yourself dominating the conversation, take a step back. Ask a reflective question. Create space for the coachee to process, respond and articulate their own thinking. This empowers them and increases ownership of the learning process.

Using Data to Strengthen Coaching

One of the most powerful tools a coach can bring to a conversation is data – specific, targetted information that captures what actually happened in the classroom.

But not all data is created equal. The most useful data is:

- agreed upon in advance (in a pre-observation conversation)
- aligned with the teacher's goals
- objective and non-judgemental
- presented clearly and specifically.

If a coach walks into a classroom with no focus, it's human nature to default to evaluation. However, if the coach and teacher have previously discussed what to observe and what data to collect, the observation becomes purposeful and supportive, but not evaluative.

Types of Data

There are a number of different ways to collect data.

- **Selective verbatim**: a word-for-word record of what students or teachers say. Such records are great for analysing questioning or dialogue.

- **Anecdotal record**: a narrative of observed events or instructional moves during a lesson.

- **Verbal flow**: a map showing who speaks to whom, and when. This information is useful for examining student participation.

- **Class traffic**: a record of movement patterns in the classroom.

- **Event count**: a tally of how often a particular behaviour or strategy occurs (e.g. wait time, student questioning).

- **Duration**: measuring how long students spend on a task or how long the teacher talks.

- **Time sampling**: a snapshot of what is happening at regular intervals (e.g. every 2 minutes).

- **Physical map**: a visual representation of room layout and activity zones.

These tools help make teaching visible. They turn the abstract into something we can observe, discuss and reflect on. They remove the veil of judgement and replace it with curiosity and clarity.

Embedding a Culture of Coaching

Coaching is not a program, but a mindset. It's a way of working. A culture.

When schools commit to coaching, they commit to growing people, not just delivering content. They commit to trust, collaboration and ongoing reflection. They create space for teachers to take risks, try new ideas and learn together.

Ultimately, coaching is not just about teacher development – it's about student success. Because when teachers grow, learners thrive.

CHAPTER 8

Culture for Success

The **Six-Step Framework** is not a one-size-fits-all program – it is a flexible structure designed to support the development of a robust and effective coaching culture within your school. The six elements are the foundational pillars of your coaching approach.

Success in coaching doesn't happen by chance. It requires intentional planning, consistent practice and a shared understanding across the school community. Each step in this framework addresses a critical component of the coaching process. If even one is neglected, the overall impact of coaching will be diminished and the goals of improving teacher practice – and ultimately, student outcomes – may not be achieved.

The framework is built on the belief that coaching should focus on building teacher capacity. When done well, coaching leads to professional growth, improved instructional practice and better learning outcomes for students.

Each of the six steps is explored in detail below.

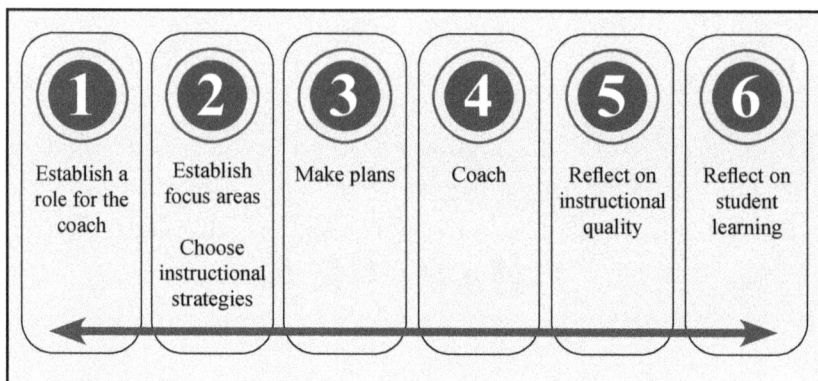

1	2	3	4	5	6
Establish a role for the coach	Establish focus areas Choose instructional strategies	Make plans	Coach	Reflect on instructional quality	Reflect on student learning

1. Establish a Role for the Coach

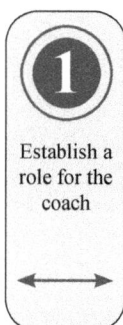

Before any effective coaching can occur, the role of the coach must be clearly defined and understood by everyone in the school community. This is the foundation upon which all other elements of the coaching program rest.

Understanding Coaching Models

The structure of instructional coaching can vary widely depending on the context and culture of the school. There is no single 'correct' model. What matters is that the model is intentional, clearly communicated and appropriate for the school's needs.

Some schools designate a few staff members as Instructional Coaches – individuals with specific expertise who work across teams or departments. Others adopt a peer coaching model, where all teachers participate as both coaches and coachees in reciprocal partnerships. In some settings, coaching may be aligned to curriculum areas, year levels or even school improvement goals.

Whatever the structure, the key is alignment with purpose. Schools must ask:

- What are we trying to achieve with coaching?
- What kind of support will best help our teachers grow?
- What model fits our current culture, resources and priorities?

While coaching models may differ, one element is absolutely non-negotiable – clarity of purpose and role.

If the role of the coach is vague or inconsistently communicated, it can breed confusion, fear and mistrust. For example, a classroom visit framed as a 'coaching observation' can feel like an informal performance review if the coach's role has not been clearly distinguished from that of an evaluator. Similarly, a reflective conversation may feel confrontational if teachers are unclear about the coach's purpose.

In the absence of clarity, teachers may begin to question the validity of the coaching. They may start asking:

- Why is this person in my classroom?
- Is this part of my appraisal?
- Will this feedback be shared with the leadership team?
- Am I being judged?

These doubts undermine the most essential ingredient of effective coaching – trust.

Trust is the bedrock of any coaching relationship. Without it, teachers are unlikely to:

- show vulnerability
- invite observation or feedback

- experiment with new instructional strategies
- reflect honestly on their practice
- learn from mistakes.

When trust is present, coaching becomes a safe space for growth. Teachers feel supported, rather than scrutinised. They are more open to constructive feedback, more willing to take risks and more likely to engage deeply in professional learning.

Establishing this level of trust requires more than just good intentions – it requires consistent messaging, confidentiality and time. Coaches must build professional relationships with their colleagues that are grounded in mutual respect, empathy and shared purpose.

Leadership Sets the Tone

Leadership plays a pivotal role in shaping the narrative around coaching. When the Principal or school leadership team consistently reinforces that coaching is about **growth, not appraisal** – about **support, not surveillance** – staff are far more likely to engage with the process in a meaningful way.

Clear messaging from leadership might include:

- staff presentations or workshops outlining the coaching model
- written documentation that defines the role and scope of the coach
- public endorsements of coaching as a professional development tool
- active modelling of a coaching mindset by school leaders themselves.

When these messages are echoed in words and actions across the school, they help establish a culture where coaching is normalised, valued and trusted.

It is important to recognise that defining the coach's role is not a one-time event. As schools grow and change, so too must the structures that support professional learning. Regularly revisiting and reaffirming the coaching role – through staff meetings, surveys, informal check-ins and reflection – is essential to maintaining clarity and trust.

As the coaching culture matures, staff may begin to co-construct aspects of the coaching process, leading to even greater ownership and investment. What begins as a defined role becomes a shared practice.

Key Takeaways

There are a number of crucial aspects to remember.

- The coach's role must be explicitly defined and consistently communicated.
- Clarity prevents coaching from being misinterpreted as performance evaluation.
- Trust is essential for coaching to be effective – and it must be actively nurtured.
- School leadership plays a critical role in reinforcing that coaching is about growth.
- The coaching role should be revisited regularly to sustain engagement and alignment.

Coaching Role Clarity Checklist

Use the checklist below to ensure your school has clearly

established instructional coaches, whose roles have been communicated.

The coaching model (e.g. expert, peer, year-level aligned) is defined and fits the school's context.

- All staff understand the purpose of coaching to be professional growth, not evaluation.

- The distinction between coaching and appraisal is clear to both coaches and coachees.

- Leadership consistently reinforces the value and safety of coaching in public and private forums.

- Coaches understand and commit to confidentiality and professionalism in all interactions.

- The coaching role is documented and accessible to all staff.

- The definition of the coaching role is reviewed and refreshed at key points during the year.

2. Establish Focus Areas and Choose Instructional Strategies

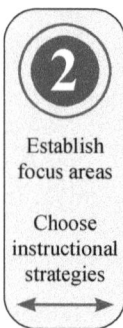

Of all the steps in an instructional coaching cycle, this one (Step 2) is arguably the most pivotal. Getting this step right sets the entire coaching relationship up for success. Getting it wrong can create confusion, tension and resistance. In this step, the coach meets with the coachee in a structured, collaborative conversation aimed at identifying both a clear focus area for improvement and specific instructional strategies the coachee is willing to try. It is essential that both elements

– **focus area** and **strategies** – are present. One without the other significantly reduces the impact of the coaching process.

Setting the Focus Area

The conversation typically begins with the identification of a focus area. This should emerge from thoughtful dialogue that is guided by questioning frameworks such as reflective questioning, appreciative inquiry or the GROW model (Goal, Reality, Options, Will). These frameworks help the coach draw out the coachee's perceptions of their teaching practice, their challenges and their aspirations. The resulting focus area might relate to classroom management, formative assessment, student engagement, instructional delivery, differentiation or another aspect of teaching practice.

The focus area should be:

- specific enough to be actionable
- relevant to the coachee's current challenges or goals
- aligned with school priorities or student needs
- important enough to justify sustained attention over time.

For example, a focus area of 'improve classroom management' is broad. A more refined focus might be 'increase student engagement during transitions by using proactive behaviour cues'.

The Critical Role of Strategy Selection

It is not sufficient, however, to just identify a focus area. One of the most common mistakes in coaching is stopping at this point, that is, walking into an observation with a general area of interest but no clear idea of what the teacher is working on within that area. When this happens, the observation becomes vague and unfocused and the feedback conversation risks turning into an evaluation of the teacher's ability rather than a collaborative exploration of instructional improvement.

To avoid this, the coach must help the coachee identify specific instructional strategies to implement as part of their improvement effort. This is where the coaching process becomes both supportive and targetted. The strategies should be:

- concrete and observable

- research-informed or evidence-based

- feasible within the teacher's current classroom context

- agreed upon by both the coach and the coachee.

Continuing with our earlier example, if the coachee identifies classroom management as their focus area, the coach might help them select two or three specific strategies to trial. These may be:

- greeting students at the door to establish a positive tone

- using proximity and non-verbal cues to manage off-task behaviour

- establishing and practising clear routines for transitions between activities.

Why This Matters: The Feedback Connection

This preparatory work becomes especially important in Step 5, when the coach provides feedback following a classroom observation. Consider the difference between these two scenarios:

- **Without specific strategies**

   The coach observes a lesson focused on 'classroom management'. If management is poor, the coach is left commenting on general behaviour or discipline issues, which can easily come across as critical or judgemental. The coachee may feel personally attacked, become defensive or shut down entirely.

- **With specific strategies**

  The coach observes how well the agreed-upon strategies were implemented. Even if classroom management is still a challenge, the feedback discussion is anchored in evaluating whether the strategies were effective, what adjustments might improve them and what to try next. The focus remains on problem-solving and growth, not on the teacher's competence or worth.

This shift transforms the tone and impact of the coaching conversation. It makes feedback:

- less personal and more objective
- more focused on improvement than evaluation
- easier to accept and apply
- more likely to lead to sustained instructional change.

Empowering the Coachee

Helping the coachee select and commit to specific strategies is empowering. It reinforces their agency and professionalism by positioning them as the decision-maker in their own growth journey. They are not being told what to do; they are choosing what to try, with support. This autonomy increases buy-in and motivation, both of which are key to sustained improvement.

Moreover, this approach normalises experimentation in the classroom. The message is not, 'You need to fix this,' but rather, 'Let's test some ideas and learn together'. This reduces the fear of failure and builds a coaching culture based on trust, curiosity and continuous learning.

In short, if a coach and coachee stop at simply naming a focus area, they short-circuit the entire process. The observation becomes a vague scan for issues rather than a purposeful investigation of strategy. The feedback becomes evaluative instead of constructive. The coachee may feel criticised instead of supported. And the opportunity for meaningful change is diminished.

But when this step is done thoroughly – when focus and strategies are both clearly defined – it strengthens every subsequent step of the coaching cycle. It creates clarity, builds trust, enhances professionalism and, most importantly, supports real improvements in teaching and learning.

An Example of a Coaching Dialogue

In the following example, we see the coach and coachee moving from 'focus area' to 'strategy'.

Context: A coach is meeting with a teacher who wants to improve classroom management. The coach uses reflective questioning to help the teacher identify both the focus area and specific strategies to try.

Coach: Thanks for taking the time to meet today. Last time we spoke, you mentioned that managing student behaviour during group work can be challenging. Would you say that's an area you'd like to focus on?

Coachee: Yes, definitely. I feel like I lose control a bit when students are working in groups. There's too much noise and I'm not always sure they're staying on task.

Coach: Okay, so we could define our focus area as *classroom management during group work*. Does that feel specific enough to you?

Coachee: Yes, that sounds right.

Coach: Great. Now, let's think about what strategies you might want to try. What have you already done to manage group behaviour?

Coachee: I've tried giving them a timer and walking around to monitor, but I'm not consistent with it.

Coach: Good start. What do you think would happen if you established clear group norms before starting and used a visible noise-level chart during the activity?

Coachee: That could help. I've seen other teachers use noise charts, but I haven't tried it myself.

Coach: Let's make those your strategies for the next lesson – 1. Set group norms at the beginning; 2. Use a noise-level chart; 3. Circulate consistently. I'll observe and look specifically at how those strategies play out. Then we can debrief and see what's working and what we can tweak. How does that sound?

Coachee: Perfect. That feels a lot more manageable.

Coaching Checklist: Establishing Focus and Strategies
Use the following checklist to ensure Step 2 is fully and effectively completed before moving on to classroom observation.

Establishing the Focus Area
- The focus area is clearly stated and understood by both coach and coachee.
- The focus is specific and actionable (e.g. 'managing group work transitions' rather than 'classroom management').
- The focus aligns with teacher needs, student outcomes or school priorities.

- The coachee feels ownership of the chosen focus area.

Identifying Instructional Strategies

- Between one and three specific strategies are identified to address the focus area.

- Strategies are research-informed, practical and observable.

- The coach and coachee have discussed the purpose of each strategy.

- The coachee is committed to trying the chosen strategies before the observation.

- The coach has documented the strategies and will use them as the lens for observation.

3. Make Plans

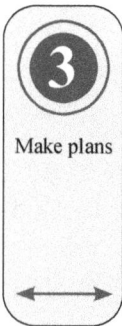

While this may be the simplest step in the coaching process, it remains critically important. During the meeting, be sure to document key elements of the conversation for future reference. This includes the focus area and instructional strategies discussed in Step 2, as well as logistical details such as dates and times for upcoming meetings, classroom observations and feedback sessions.

Make plans

Documenting these elements shows a mutual commitment to the coaching process. It signals that this work is meaningful – not just another item on a checklist. Demonstrating the value you place on the process builds trust and supports long-term success.

Be mindful, however, to keep the documentation simple. If the process becomes overly complex, it can detract from meaningful dialogue and reduce active listening. The goal is to engage with the coachee, not to fill out forms.

Finally, honour the schedule you've set. Frequent cancellations or rescheduling can undermine the coaching relationship by signalling that it is not a priority. Consistency and following through are essential to maintaining trust and momentum.

Coaching Conversation Template

Here is an example of a simple template for a coaching conversation. The coach and coachee can use this to record their discussions.

Coach: _____

Coachee: _____

Date of Meeting: _____

Time: _____

Location / Modality (in-person, virtual): _____

1. Focus Area

What is the primary focus for this coaching cycle or conversation?

_____

_____

2. Instructional Strategies

Which instructional strategies were discussed or will be implemented to address the focus area?

_____

_____

3. Scheduled Actions and Commitments

Outline dates and times for observations, follow-up meetings or feedback sessions.

Activity	Date	Time	Notes
Classroom Observation	_____	_____	_____ _____
Feedback Session	_____	_____	_____ _____
Next Coaching Conversation	_____	_____	_____ _____

4. Notes and Reflections

Key points from the discussion, coachee insights or areas to revisit later.

_____

_____

5. Action Steps

What specific steps will the coach and coachee take before the next meeting?

- _____
  _____

- _____
  _____

- _____
  _____

4. Coach

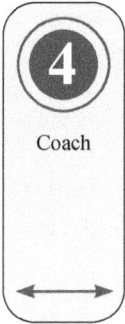

By the time a coaching relationship has progressed through the first three steps – clarifying roles, determining focus area and strategies and committing to a shared plan – the foundation is firmly in place. At this point, both coach and coachee have a clear understanding of the purpose and direction of their work together. The coach's role is well-defined; the focus areas have evolved into tangible strategies; and the documentation process has captured a commitment to growth. Now comes an important phase – selecting how the coaching will take place.

This is where flexibility and responsiveness are essential. While classroom observation and data collection are often considered the cornerstone of instructional coaching, they are just **one** of many possible approaches. It's easy for both coaches and coachees to fall into the trap of thinking there's a 'correct' way to do coaching – usually, this involves the coach observing the teacher and giving feedback. While this model is effective in many contexts, it is not universally applicable or necessary.

We must remain grounded in our central purpose – **to support teacher growth in a way that leads to improved student outcomes**. That may happen through observation and feedback, but it can also occur through reflective dialogue, collaborative teaching or teacher-led inquiry. What matters most is not the method, but the impact.

Coaching Approaches

There are a number of common and effective coaching approaches that extend beyond classroom observation.

- **Team teaching**

  Coach and coachee plan and teach together, offering opportunities for real-time collaboration and modelling.

- **Co-teaching**

  Similar to team teaching, but often with more equal responsibility and shared decision-making during instruction.

- **In-class modelling**

  The coach demonstrates a specific strategy or approach while the teacher observes, then they debrief and reflect.

- **Modelling without students**

  Particularly helpful when teachers want to focus on pedagogy or instructional delivery without the complexity of student interaction.

- **Observing other teachers**

  Teachers visit colleagues' classrooms (sometimes with the coach) to gather new ideas and reflect on different styles and strategies.

- **Video analysis**

  The teacher records a lesson and reviews it, either independently or with the coach, to identify strengths and areas for development.

- **Reflective conversations**

  Regular, purposeful dialogue that encourages teachers to think deeply about their practice, test new ideas and reflect on impact.

Each of these methods has its own value and can be powerful depending on the context. Coaches should work with teachers to select the approach – or combination of approaches – that best aligns with their needs, goals and comfort level. Offering choice is a way of respecting the professionalism of the teacher and reinforcing that coaching is a collaborative process.

An Example

Let me share an example that challenged my own assumptions about what effective coaching can look like.

An experienced senior science teacher asked me to be his coach. To be honest, I felt a bit intimidated. He was already an outstanding teacher with years of experience and science was not my area of expertise. I wondered what I could offer him. But coaching isn't about being the expert in content – it's about facilitating growth – so we began. Our first meeting focused on clarifying his goals, which he had already been thinking about in some detail.

*From there, our coaching took the shape of **fortnightly reflective conversations**. He would share what he was experimenting with in the classroom and together we would unpack what was working, what needed adjustment and why certain strategies seemed more effective than others. I didn't observe a single lesson. Instead, I listened, asked questions, challenged his thinking (at times) and helped him clarify his own reflections.*

At the end of the term, I asked him two critical questions:

- *Do you feel your teaching has improved as a result of our coaching conversations?*
- *How do you know?*

Without hesitation, he answered yes to the first question. He was then able to clearly identify specific changes in his instructional practice, improvements in student engagement and performance and areas where he had grown in confidence and clarity. He spoke with ownership and insight about his development and, importantly, about the impact on his students.

This experience was a turning point for me as a coach. It reminded me that effective coaching is not about following a script or checklist. It's about recognising that different teachers need different things at different times. Some thrive when the coach is present in the classroom, modelling or observing. Others grow most when they are given space to reflect and process independently, supported by thoughtful conversation. There is no one-size-fits-all approach.

At the very beginning of this book, we established that our core purpose is to support teacher growth with the ultimate aim of improving student learning. This example highlights that powerful growth can happen without direct classroom involvement from the coach. In this case, the teacher's commitment, reflective capacity and willingness to trial new strategies were the engine of his improvement. I simply provided the space, structure and encouragement he needed to move forward.

Coaching is not about control or oversight. It's about partnership, adaptability and trust. Trust in the process. Trust in the teacher. And trust in the idea that growth looks different for everyone.

Key Takeaways

There are a number of important things to remember.

- Coaching methods should be tailored to the teacher's goals, context and preferences.

- Classroom observation is valuable, but not always necessary.

- A menu of coaching options empowers teachers and honours their agency.

- Reflective conversations can be just as powerful as in-class involvement.

- The focus should always remain on teacher growth for student success.

- Flexibility and trust are the foundations of a responsive coaching relationship.

5. Reflect on Instructional Quality

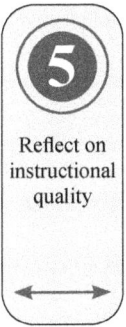

The post-coaching conversation is often where the most significant professional learning occurs. This is the time when educators are encouraged to slow down, think deeply and make meaning of their recent instructional experiences. Coaches play a crucial role in facilitating this reflection by carefully crafting thoughtful, open-ended questions that prompt genuine insight. The aim is to help the coachee reflect not only on what happened, but why it happened, how it felt and what it meant for student learning.

A vital part of this conversation involves reviewing any data or notes gathered during the classroom observation. This might include student work samples, observation checklists, anecdotal records or even video footage. The coach shares what they observed regarding the use of the specific instructional strategies that were identified and agreed upon earlier in the process, during Step 2. These observations are framed in a non-judgemental way, with the goal of promoting curiosity, dialogue and learning rather than evaluation.

Importantly, the coachee is invited to share their own reflections. How did it feel to implement a new or refined instructional approach? What surprised them? What seemed to work well? What didn't go as expected?

When the earlier steps of the coaching process have been intentional and collaborative, feedback becomes more productive and less threatening. Because the strategies under discussion were jointly explored and chosen, the teacher is more likely to feel ownership over their learning. This makes the coach's feedback feel like a natural continuation of a shared inquiry rather than an external judgement.

Impact

This reflective phase also includes critical questions about impact:

- Was the strategy effective in improving student outcomes?
- Did it influence student engagement, behaviour or achievement?
- How did the students respond?
- Were there visible shifts in the classroom dynamic?
- Is the teacher feeling more confident and capable as a result of trying this new approach?

As these questions are unpacked, both the coach and coachee begin to form a clearer picture of what is working, what might need adjustment and what deserves further investigation. This marks the beginning of a continuous improvement cycle – a hallmark of high-quality professional learning. It also opens the door to new ideas and possibilities. Together, coach and coachee can ask:

- Should we continue refining this strategy?
- Is it time to try a new approach?
- Are there different goals we want to pursue based on what we've learned?

Celebrate Progress

Celebrating progress is also a crucial part of this conversation. Taking time to acknowledge what has gone well helps to build momentum and sustain motivation. Even small wins – trying something new, noticing a slight change in student behaviour or feeling more confident about a particular teaching move – are worth recognising. Affirming the teacher's efforts reinforces their professional identity and highlights the value of their on-going commitment to learning.

Next Steps

Finally, the coach and coachee discuss the next steps. Depending on the needs and preferences of the teacher, the coaching relationship may continue with regular meetings, or it might shift into a different rhythm. Perhaps the teacher wants to try out the strategy more independently before checking in again. Maybe new goals have emerged from the reflection process. There is no one-size-fits-all schedule at this stage. The path forward should be flexible, responsive and driven by the coachee's evolving needs and aspirations.

By thoughtfully engaging in this reflective process, instructional coaching becomes more than just a series of check-ins

– it becomes a dynamic, empowering partnership grounded in trust, curiosity and a shared commitment to improving teaching and learning.

6. Reflect on Student Learning

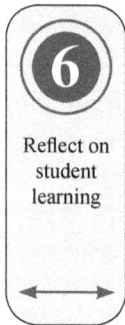

At the heart of every educator's work is a singular, powerful motivator – student growth. Whether this growth is an increase in confidence, a spark of creativity, stronger self-regulation or improved academic achievement, witnessing a student thrive is one of the most rewarding aspects of teaching. It is this sense of purpose – the belief we are making a difference – that fuels teachers through the challenges and complexities of the classroom.

Instructional coaching can deepen this sense of impact when it intentionally connects teaching practice to student outcomes. This is a crucial step in the coaching process, and one that can transform how a teacher views their own development. Coaches play a key role in helping teachers pause, step back and reflect – not only on how they are changing professionally, but on how those changes are positively influencing their students.

Sometimes the link between teacher practice and student learning is obvious – perhaps a new questioning technique sparks deeper classroom discussions or a revised lesson structure results in clearer student understanding. But often, in the rush of daily teaching, these connections are easy to miss. Teachers can become so focused on perfecting their own delivery or managing the demands of the classroom that they overlook the very impact they are having on student growth.

This is where the coach's perspective becomes invaluable. A

coach can shine a light on the evidence of student learning – whether it is visible in assessment results, classroom behaviours, student reflections or subtle shifts in engagement. By drawing attention to these indicators, coaches help coachees see that their efforts are not just theoretical or procedural – they are making a real, measurable difference in the lives of their students.

These conversations help shift the narrative around coaching. Instead of being perceived as an obligation or an evaluative process, coaching becomes a gift – a professional opportunity to do what teachers already love, but with greater effectiveness and clarity. When teachers begin to see that coaching is not about fixing deficits, but about magnifying their strengths and extending their reach, their mindset shifts. Coaching becomes less about compliance and more about empowerment.

Questions for Reflection Sessions

To support this, coaches can ask powerful, student-centred questions during reflection sessions:

- What changes have you noticed in your students since implementing this strategy?
- Are students more engaged, confident or independent?
- Have learning outcomes improved? If so, in what ways?
- How are students responding emotionally and socially?
- What student successes are you most proud of?

The purpose of these questions isn't to collect data for evaluation but to foster awareness and celebration. Even small shifts in student behaviour or learning should be acknowledged. Every success story – no matter how minor it may seem – reinforces the value of instructional growth and affirms the teacher's purpose.

Moreover, these reflections help guide the next steps in the coaching process. If a strategy has clearly led to positive student outcomes, it might be worth exploring further or embedding more deeply into regular practice. If the results are mixed, the coach and coachee can discuss adjustments, alternatives or new directions. In either case, the guiding question remains – what is best for students?

Ultimately, keeping student learning at the centre of the coaching conversation ensures that professional growth is always tied to its true purpose. It reinforces the idea that every decision a teacher makes in their own development is, at its core, a decision made for their students. When this alignment is clear, coaching becomes more than just professional support – it becomes a moral and instructional compass that helps educators do their best work for those who need it most.

CONCLUSION

Empowering Educators Through Mentoring and Coaching

At its core, education is a people-centred profession rooted in relationships, continuous growth and a shared commitment to student success. Throughout this book, we have explored the foundations, practices and frameworks that make mentoring and coaching not only powerful tools for teacher development, but essential components of a thriving school culture.

We began by examining why schools should invest in mentoring and coaching. In an era of increasing complexity and accountability, educators need more than policies and programs. They need personalised support, meaningful collaboration and trusted partnerships that enable them to grow with purpose. Mentoring and coaching provide this, offering structured yet flexible avenues for professional reflection, feedback and goal setting.

By clearly defining the differences between mentoring and coaching, we've highlighted the unique contributions of each approach. Mentoring offers guidance, wisdom and reassurance

– particularly for early career teachers navigating the challenges of the profession. Coaching, on the other hand, invites inquiry, promotes instructional experimentation and fosters a deep sense of agency and ownership over one's practice.

We've also explored the skills and dispositions required to be an effective mentor or coach – empathy, active listening, strategic questioning and a commitment to both professional standards and individual teacher growth. These roles are not about having all the answers but about creating the conditions in which educators feel safe to take risks, reflect honestly and strive for excellence.

Throughout this book, we've returned to the importance of **conversations** and looked at how they can be structured through frameworks like ROID and GROW. We've considered how these conversations must be centred on trust, curiosity and shared purpose. Whether supporting an early career teacher through a school-wide mentoring program or engaging in a reflective coaching cycle focused on student learning, the quality of dialogue shapes the quality of development.

Most importantly, we've reinforced the idea that **everything we do as mentors and coaches must ultimately serve students**. When teachers grow, students benefit. When we help educators reflect on their instruction, adapt their strategies and deepen their impact, we contribute directly to improved student engagement, wellbeing and achievement.

Mentoring and coaching are not 'extras' to be added to an already full plate – they *are* the plate. They are the foundation upon which professional learning, teacher wellbeing and educational excellence are built. When implemented thoughtfully and systematically, they have the power to transform not just individual teachers but entire school cultures.

As you move forward, I hope the tools, ideas and strategies shared in this book inspire action, spark meaningful conversations and deepen your commitment to supporting every educator to be the very best they can be – for themselves, for their colleagues and, most importantly, for their students.

REFERENCES

Broadwell, M. M. (1969). The Four Levels of Teaching. *Gospel Guardian, 20*(41).

Costa, A. L., & Garmston, R. J. (2016). *Cognitive coaching: Developing self-directed leaders and learners* (3rd ed.). Rowman & Littlefield.

Davey, J. (2018, April 27). *The Marigold Effect*. YouTube. https://www.youtube.com/watch?v=Ky9t5VGG-gM

Downey, M. (2003). *Effective coaching: lessons from the coaches' coach*. Texere.

Gonzalez, J. (2017, October 12). *Find Your Marigold: The One Essential Rule for New Teachers | Cult of Pedagogy*. Cult of Pedagogy. https://www.cultofpedagogy.com/marigolds/

Shaw, G. B. (n.d.). *The single biggest problem in communication is the illusion that it has taken place*. Attributed quote.

Whitmore, J. (2002). *Coaching for Performance : GROWing people, Performance and Purpose* (3rd ed.). Nicholas Brealey.

Wise, K. (2010). *Coaching is about enabling individuals to make conscious decisions and empowering them to become leaders in their own lives*. Unpublished.

To find out more about Jodie Davey and the courses she offers through Powerful Partnerships, visit her website

https://www.powerfulpartnerships.com.au/

or contact Jodie directly at

jodie@powerfulpartnerships.com.au

www.ingramcontent.com/pod-product-compliance
Lightning Source LLC
Chambersburg PA
CBHW052012030426
42334CB00029BA/3198